BOX

SUE D. BURTON

Winner of the Two Sylvias Press 2017 Poetry Book Prize

Two Sylvias Press

Two Sylvias Press
PO Box 1524
Kingston, WA 98346
twosylviaspress@gmail.com

Cover Art: Caitlin Keogh
Cover Design (front): W. David Powell
Cover Design (back): Kelli Russell Agodon
Book Design: Annette Spaulding-Convy
Author Photo: Alison Prine
Contest Judge: Diane Seuss

Cover Art: Caitlin Keogh, *Study for Interiors*, 2016, Graphite and colored pencil on paper, 16 1/2 x 11 3/4 in (42 x 29.8 cm), Image: Courtesy of the artist and Bortolami, New York.

Created with the belief that *great writing is good for the world*, Two Sylvias Press mixes modern technology, classic style, and literary intellect with an eco-friendly heart. We draw our inspiration from the poetic literary talent of Sylvia Plath and the editorial business sense of Sylvia Beach. We are an independent press dedicated to publishing the exceptional voices of writers.

For more information about Two Sylvias Press please visit:
www.twosylviaspress.com

First Edition. Created in the United States of America.

ISBN: 978-1-948767-02-6

Two Sylvias Press
www.twosylviaspress.com

Praise for *Box*

Let's just get this part out of the way, Sue Burton's *Box* is a brilliant, imperative, masterful collection. I envy this book; I covet and adore it. It is a book of the body and the soul, of the body as a trap for the soul, and the box—from the magician's box, where the body is sawn in half, to the coffin—as a trap for the (female) body. It is a book of mirth and snark—with all-caps titles like "WHY I'M NOT COMING TO MY FUNERAL," "MY NARRATIVE BENT IS BENT ON TELLING A STORY," and "OVER AT THE SHIVA PIANO LOUNGE THE WOMAN WHO WAS SAWN IN HALF IS DRINKING A HIPSTER VARIANT (GREEN CHARTREUSE AND GIN) OF LYDIA E. PINKHAM'S 1876 ORIGINAL VEGETABLE COMPOUND"—and deadly serious intent. If the box is its defining metaphor, and the sawed-in-half-woman its central archetype, then its thematic axis is abortion, legal, illegal, botched, and died-for. Burton's source material is the dovetailing of the holy quartet: public history, political history, family history, and apparently personal history. But this is poetry, not polemic. Its bottom line is the possibility of language within and beyond the borders of its ideas. Along with being badass and defiant and imaginative as hell, the book is formally-astute and deeply literary. There is a villanelle. There are sonnets, including a prose sonnet sequence in which each poem is shaped like—you guessed it—a box. And there is Hopkins, Dickinson, Marianne Moore, and Adrienne Rich canoodling in the same collection with a girl named Ruby, a sprite, "dressed like a man dressed like a goat...down there in the dark like Nijinsky's faun, in a cream-colored body suit, little goat horns that nobody could see, bobby-pinned in hair that nobody could see, red-streaked and kinked." It's all here—story, song, and figuration, insurgence, sorrow, and love. "Once a woman sawn in half, always./Though it's all in the eye—yours—the beholder," she writes. I beheld. I urge you, too, to behold.
　—**Diane Seuss** (Contest Judge)

❦

According to her poems, and I don't doubt it in the least, Sue Burton has a sign saying *Don't Bore God* on her study wall. Not a problem—God could not possibly be bored by these intrepid poems, which range broadly across experience, by turns worldly, spiritually plaintive, self-interrogating and wry. All are written with an acute, spiritual practicality and a fierce sense of the mortal predicament.

    —Tony Hoagland

℘

Sue Burton's *Box* is a book we need: brave, bold, inventive, magical. Deftly braiding personal and political, social history and contemporary concerns, the factual and the fantastical, *Box* illuminates what it means to be she *who is sawn in half* and she who steps out of that box to confront the mayhem where, indeed, "some fanatic is packing a gun." Along with Burton's keen ear for the music and muscle of the poem, there's tenderness, passion, transcendence, humor, and dead-on serious intent. As she writes, "the Magic of course, I always say, is not/ in being sawn in half, but in rebirth/ Climbing back onstage night after night..." These poems show us that magic, of climbing back on stage here in "America, in fine fettle/while the fields burn." At the end of "A Matter of the Soul" Burton asks, "Do I dare write this poem?" Thankfully yes, she did write the poem—these poems, this brilliant new book.

    —Carol Potter

℘

Sue Burton's moving, riveting *Box* is a tour de force of documenting, conjuring, voicing. Women across centuries linked by history, abortion, violence, dubious magic and encounters with the soul, are evoked with knife-perfect language and inventive poetic strategies that hold the reader to the crucial task of witnessing. An unforgettable book.

    —Robin Behn

Acknowledgments

My thanks to the editors of the following publications where these poems, sometimes in different versions, originally appeared:

Beloit Poetry Journal: "Bulletproof"; "Letter from Antoinette Bope to Her Sister Mabel, May 24, 1902"; "Virtue a Lily, but Pennyroyal Being Practical"

Blackbird: "The Woman Who Is To Be Sawn in Half"; "All in All, Another Productive Day in the Thicket of Disappointment"; and "The Woman Who is Sawn in Half Thinks about Elephants: Marianne Moore Feeding them Bread at the Circus & Houdini who Made One Disappear (& was Not 'Uncomfortably Popular' with them as was Miss Moore)"

The Comstock Review: "Paring Knife" (as "The History of the Paring Knife") and "My Narrative Bent Is Bent on Telling a Story" (as "Eugenia's Narrative Bent is Bent on Telling a Story")

5 AM: "On This Matter of the Soul"

Fourth Genre: "Box Set" (awarded *Fourth Genre*'s 2017 Steinberg Prize)

Green Mountains Review: "Why I'm Not Coming to My Funeral" and "The Abortionist Goes to the Grocery Store"

GMR Online: "The House of Illusion"; "Why Am I Lying in a Box?": "Ruby"; and "After Hours, the Box (All Lacquer & Gold Locks) Foretells:"

Harvard Review: "Let Us Consider Julia"

Hayden's Ferry Review: "Today I Must Write My Obituary"

Hunger Mountain: "I Decide to Come Back, Next Life," (as "Eugenia Decides to Come Back, Next Life,")

Midway Journal: "Once a God Painted His Skin Blue, Like the Sky, to be Invisible above the Battlefield"

New Haven Review: "Over at the Shiva Piano Lounge The Woman Who Was Sawn in Half Is Drinking a Hipster Variant (Green Chartreuse and Gin) of Lydia E. Pinkham's 1876 Original Vegetable Compound"

New Ohio Review: "Should I Take It as a Sign"

Shenandoah: "The Woman Who Is To Be Sawn in Half Reveals the Secret of Her Dying Art"

Spillway: "American Pastoral"

Water~Stone Review: "Ringling Bros: Mother & Daughter, Funeral Procession"

Many thanks to Faith Adiele for selecting my lyric essay "Box Set" for *Fourth Genre*'s 2017 Steinberg Prize (Vol. 20, No. 1, Spring 2018, pp 1-8).

A longer version of "Letter from Antoinette Bope to Her Sister Mabel, May 24, 1902" is included in the anthology *Forgotten Women: A Tribute in Poetry* (Grayson Books, 2017).

"American Pastoral" is included in the anthology *Birchsong, Poetry Centered in Vermont*, v. II. (Blueline Press, 2018).

"Why I'm Not Coming to My Funeral" was featured on *Verse Daily* and has been printed as a letterpress broadside (The Center for Book Arts, 2011).

"Bulletproof" was nominated by *Beloit Poetry Journal* for a Pushcart.

"Once a God Painted His Skin Blue, Like the Sky, to be Invisible above the Battlefield" was nominated by *Midway Journal* for the Best of the Net Anthology.

Thank you to the Vermont Arts Council, a State agency with funding from the National Endowment of the Arts, for support during the completion of this work.

A special thank you to Diane Seuss, for putting her wild and wise (and enviable!) poetry out into the world and for selecting *BOX* for the Two Sylvias Press 2017 book award (the *Four-Legged Girl* recognizes the *Woman Sawn in Half*). And, oh my goodness, thank you to Two Sylvias Press editors Kelli Russell Agodon and Annette Spaulding-Convy for their unflagging enthusiasm and support. It's been a joy to work with them.

Thank you to Caitlin Keogh and the Bortolami Gallery for Caitlin's incredible *Study for Interiors* and to W. David Powell for his inspired design work.

And, YES!, thank you to my dear poet friends: without you, *BOX* would not exist. Hooray for the Pine Street Poets: Marylen Grigas, Alison Prine, Joan White; for PO: Marylen Grigas (!), Angela Patten, Anna Blackmer, Judy Chalmer, Florence McCloud, Alison Moncrief Bromage, Emily Skoler, Liz Powell, Adrie Kusserow; and for Carol Westberg, Anne Damrosch, Clyde Watson, Nora Mitchell, Daniel Lusk, Sharon Webster. And a big round of applause for Carol Potter, poetry-midwife *par excellance*!

Last, but not least, my love and gratitude to my "better half"—my husband Jan Schultz.

Table Of Contents

for Jan

I

THE ABORTIONIST GOES TO THE GROCERY STORE

I wheel my cart around. I don't look
at the cabbages and say, Isn't there a thing
about cabbages and babies?

I *hi there* my neighbors, like everybody.
I study the backs of cereal boxes.

This is a political poem.

I'm the one who winces at the title.
I don't want to poke fun.
I like to blend in.

At my age, why should it matter?
I do blend in.
Yes? No?

Once—always once,
there was a maiden.

BULLETPROOF

Today it's Hopkins and *his obscure spiritual contraptions*—
everything I read is heart-corseted, like a concealable vest,
police surplus good as new. Some fanatic is packing a gun.

I turn to Hopkins—*living speech*—sprung,
stressed, compressed—then I'm off again, help me, obsessed.
O, restless mind—my own strange spiritual contraption.

Armor with a warranty: order it online—unless you're a felon.
But a killer aims at your head when you're his holy pretext.
Right to choose: third eye, bull's-eye. Some fanatic is packing a
        gun.

Why is the body so feared, its physicality, its passion?
Even Hopkins—*the beauty of the body is dangerous*—wrestling
with God, that obscure spiritual contraption.

Last week I read we're wired for God: blessed evolution.
We're (spring me!) wired to control—oil, water, sex.
God help us: tonight a fanatic is packing a gun.

Another doctor shot. The killer thinks he's won.
Bodies, ourselves—mere rhetoric? Beauty *is* the spirit fleshed.
I mourn, I get ready for work, I put on my contraption,
it presses on my heart. Some fanatic is packing a gun.

ON REMEMBERING THE ORDER OF THE UNIVERSE
AND THE ROADS TO HEAVEN AND HELL

It did not begin in the heart,
but the cathedral.
I remember the clacking of my heels. The cold.

The cathedral has ledges. Triggers
for the memory. *Things*. That reveal
the intentions of the soul. Silky
red threads on a curtain.

Last year I went back to see Simone. I thought
if she could read the future, she could read the past.
But everything was off.

The first time I saw her, she asked
if my husband was a hunter. She saw
a loaded gun. She said I had to take it
out of the house before I went to the place
with the palm trees.

I hate the heat.
I didn't even know there was a loaded gun.
He'd left it propped in the closet.
The dog had been barking in the field
the night before. He'd gone out,
and then he'd left it loaded in the closet.

It was late October.
Or November.
The branches were bare. Witches' brooms.
It was our last year—I knew that then.
I didn't even know there was a loaded gun.

When I am alone talking to
myself, with a glass of wine in my hand,

my right shoulder dipping forward,
who am I appeasing?

I hadn't wanted to get married in the church.
I hadn't wanted to get married.
The ring was from a hock shop.
The mind, too, has ledges.
On the way to City Hall to get the license,
I wrenched my ankle.

I suppose she might as easily have said,
You will take a long journey.
I remember the clacking of my heels.

*AS MAGICIANS MADE OBJECTS, ELEPHANTS, & PEOPLE DEFY
THE LAWS OF PHYSICS, THEY SHOWED AUDIENCES THERE
WAS NO NEED TO BE TRAPPED BY THE BODY*

— Lyn Gallacher

Drapes in my mother's house—big roses
& wisteria—drapes I hid behind, in the room
with the elephant.

The first law: Inertia.

How *did* Houdini make Jennie the elephant disappear?
Mirrors? Velvet curtains?

One day, the body will no longer trap
our great yearning.

One day, the great divide—

even if you're already sawn in half
& have nothing to lose—

THE WOMAN WHO IS TO BE SAWN IN HALF REVEALS THE SECRET OF HER DYING ART

(*line breaks deliberate*)

contort yourself, my dear, into the container—
into your contraption—do a little *shape-change*—

like my mother who at the wake became her coffin
(at which I'd stared and stared so as not to think of her inside)

roses my offering on her lid
petals, jar

(*the poem as self-storage unit*)

(O, they will conflate you
with her smile, painted or not)

but here's a secret—a woodcutter, a wolf,
the history of clinging to innocence in America

and another—the heartbeat inside the chest

(*believe it: the illusion of art everlasting*)

(*the coffin your friend*)

OVER AT THE SHIVA PIANO LOUNGE THE WOMAN WHO WAS SAWN IN HALF IS DRINKING A HIPSTER VARIANT (GREEN CHARTREUSE AND GIN) OF LYDIA E. PINKHAM'S 1876 ORIGINAL VEGETABLE COMPOUND

I do like a green Lydia after work. Though sometimes,
I don't know, Lydia kicks me.

This afternoon, at the matinee, when they lifted me
into the box, I pulled my knees up to my chest (that's
how it works—another woman dressed in red
crawls up from underneath—the saw
slices between us)—

anyway, when I tucked my knees,
I thought of myself as a shirt. A shirt being folded
and put in a suitcase. The suitcase was brown,
tweedy, lined with tan silk. The shirt was white.

Then I thought of myself as a nightgown.
A white nightgown. My great-aunt Nettie's.
The one they told her to bring to the appointment.
So to protect her clothes.

The thing about the Pinkham formula, all those roots
(life root, unicorn root, black cohosh)—
they're *emmenagogues*—they bring on your period.
So you got pep and a cure (18% alcohol
for your *womanly Complaints and Weaknesses*),
and you weren't pregnant anymore.
Except for Nettie.

She needed an appointment.

When my mother died, the undertaker gave her
a *nice blue nightgown* for the coffin.
But Nettie's was a white nightgown. No frills.

7

WHY AM I LYING IN A BOX?

Because it fits me
like a ruby slipper.

Because taking up snakes is illegal
in every state but West Virginia.

The box is my gift horse.
Don't look it in the mouth.

But what if being sawn in half
makes nothing happen?

(What if I click my heels?
What if I click three times?)

I'm deathly afraid
of death by regret

and of the mad and their lousy
weather.

THE HOUSE OF ILLUSION

She'd say, *Someday you'll go on without me*. She worked the back of the box. From underneath. Where the saw couldn't reach. Her name was Ruby. We had nothing in common but our long skinny feet. She was down there in the dark like Nijinsky's faun, in a cream-colored body suit, little goat horns that nobody could see, bobby-pinned in hair that nobody could see, red-streaked and kinked. And of course the silver shoes, same size as mine, at the end of the box—that everybody *could* see. She was always talking down there—*I'm inside Nijinsky's dead brain*. She'd get louder when Jack started with the saw. *Inside the cloven soul*. The whole box thumping like a séance. Jack sawing away, *Shut her the hell up*. But how?—that voice splitting me like a headache. It got so I didn't know who I was. She was—I don't know—a sprite. Dressed like a man dressed as a goat. She'd say, *It's magic*. And I'd think, I'm not real either, up here now with my own skinny feet out the end of a box—and a lipstick smile like the all-American prom queen. After the show, she'd perch on the bar in her faun leotard and hold up her drink—always something tall and purple or blue, with maraschinos and crushed ice—and she'd say, *It's art*.

LITTLE BLACK DRESS

I see no reason to wear red. I'm going for glam. Slinky, slit up the side. In the pocket, honeycakes for the three-headed dog. Or satin, with a ruffle-layered skirt so I can tuck my legs even in the after-ether. Tango. Once a woman sawn in half, always. Though it's all in the eye—*yours*—the beholder. Or maybe in some cosmic oculus. My mother got married in a black satin dress. She ran off and didn't tell *her* mother—it was her best dress—*marry in black, wish yourself back*—but of course I'm not getting married. *Marry in red, wish yourself dead*—whoever planted this stuff in my brain? O, do me up in an onyx-beaded bodice. And Chantilly lace pinned at the shoulder with a rare "Brenda Starr" black orchid—a token of notice from the Mystery Man. Remember him? I mean, do I have to be glum? But I don't like it that Jack looks me in the eye when he picks up the saw.

I DECIDE TO COME BACK, NEXT LIFE,

as a cocktail. A Marilyn Monroe of a drink. Plum
lipstick, see-through skirt. Yes! I love
being irresistible. *Drink me, drink me*. But
which to become?—a martini with
blue curacao & lemon twisties
or champagne with creme Yvette (aromatic
seeds, wild violets, brandy), dashed
with cloves. O, life is such
an adventure: today's Installment: a librarian
with the transplanted heart of a biker
starts to crave beef &—true
story—goes out & buys
a Harley. My drink
is the color of a heart, has cravings:
Serialized romances. Card tricks. Anchovies.
Would you *drink me, drink me* if I'm
infused with violets?—
petals tickling your throat, O,
O, it's metaphysical, the night sky
fizzing. Stars like gold canaries: cognac,
chartreuse. The cadence of the moon,
all that. Frog song.
I'm the story you'll pick up &
never put down. *You will become thirsty.*

II

LETTER FROM ANTOINETTE BOPE TO HER SISTER MABEL, MAY 24, 1902

—Antoinette Bope, 1880-1902

Oh, Mabel, *that*
that I feared.

Have found a Mrs. Beatty.
Rickety stairs up & up,
five pine chairs & a picture of Jesus.

She poked my belly through my dress
& took my money & said, come back
on the morrow—

Mabel, the morrow
is upon me.

Fear, I am dizzy.

God has slacked
his Grip.
        Rickety Stairs, railings
corded with rags, have
Mercy on me.

Yet how can Sin be raveled from the Soul?

Mrs. Beatty has a chipped
tooth. Though my landlady says—
oh, by all accounts, she's—

if only—but, Mabel,
what *other*?

VIRTUE A LILY, BUT PENNYROYAL BEING PRACTICAL

—Culpeper's Complete Herbal, 1650

Boiled and drank, provokes womens' courses.

Rundled, bitter purple herb.

Grows big by the wayside (run-by-the-ground,

flee-away). Here in Suffolk trapped in gardens.

With vinegar, abates the marks of blows about the eyes.

Helps the cold griefs of the joints.

Carminative. Diaphoretic. Also called witch weed.

Ought not to be taken if pregnant.

Squaw mint, stinking balm.

Weeks of icy rain, hay moldering in the fields.

Oh, to be you, cousin, running wild all the way to London.

ON THIS MATTER OF THE SOUL

which is not matter,
though according to the ancients
it lives in the heart or the liver;
to the Irish, in the armpit
in the shape of a fish
and is *not to be entirely trusted.*

Today I sit in a pew
in the Pearl Street Church, next
to three old friends—
our colleague George Tiller
has been shot.

No reason to be afraid—the four
of us retired—no reason—
four old abortionists in a row.
Bing, bing, bing, bing.

In Saxony the soul ran
from the mouth of the deceased
in the form of a mouse.
Celtic women got pregnant
by swallowing fly-souls.

The Egyptians had seven souls:
Ba, a bird, flies in and out
of the tomb; *khaibut* is
the shadow.

At the North Avenue clinic
we didn't go into the lab at night—
shadows on the ceiling.

The third canon of the Council
of Nantes ruled that women
have no souls.

George Tiller's patients begged him
to help—the way his father had. He didn't
know his father did abortions.

George Tiller shot dead in his church—
Sunday, May 31, 2009.
Wichita, Kansas, 10:00 a.m.
Standing in the vestibule.

Shot, the gunman said, *to save
unborn souls*.

According to Aquinas,
a man's testicles hold the souls
of his future children.

The She-Wolf gave three souls
to her son, the king of Rome.
He was killed three times.

George Tiller was shot three times,
in 1993 shot once in each arm,
in 2009 shot in the head.

Had he worn his bulletproof vest
to church? He had a boyish face.
Glasses, buzz cut. Wore a button
on his lapel, *Trust Women*.

Today at the Pearl Street Church,
a eulogy, author anonymous. Not safe
to give our names. Do I dare
write this poem?

AMERICAN PASTORAL

Autumn. House-of-no-need. Death
at the door, and you drowsing

in the sun. O, rocking chair,
rocking chair, freckles,

cornstalk hair.
House-of-no-seed-corn-drying.

So many lacquered
afternoons, and now another.

Bees, bees, why bother
massing on the goldenrod?

Ah, America—in fine fettle
while the fields burn.

AFTER HOURS, THE BOX (ALL LACQUER & GOLD LOCKS) FORETELLS:

—the monarchy, to survive, must put on a show for the people

Lo! The future has five sides & a lid.
On the top of the lid is painted *Curtains*,
on the underside, *Sky*.

Sky a Magritte blue, like an empty coat.
Ache persistent as a battlefield.

My mama was a gypsy wagon, my papa
a pine box draped with a flag.

As is, always was, ever will be.

(Once, I watched the gypsies carry the saint
down to the sea. I was a baby, & they
wrapped me in flowers & a sequined shawl.)

I'll show you, the king said. But I saw *his* fate
in the bottom of his cup.

Lo! The populace will vote in a new king.
Lo! He will provide for us another war.

ONCE A GOD PAINTED HIS SKIN BLUE, LIKE THE SKY, TO BE INVISIBLE ABOVE THE BATTLEFIELD

—Amun, the Egyptian god who is invoked at the end of Jewish and Christian prayers

I'd paint myself red. Like Gabriel's copper-tinted wings
    in the window at Basilique Saint-Denis.
            The light would pass through me
& I'd color—I'd change—everything.

        The magic of course, I always say, is not
    in being sawn in half, but in the rebirth.
            Climbing back onstage night after night.
        The ritual of it all.

Or I'd paint myself red like Matisse's red room—
            to plant an idea.
    Something like that, he said something like that.

                Or maybe the red in Picasso's Girl
    before a Mirror, where the red holding the mirror
            is the color of the box—my box—
    my twin curled up inside.

            There is always another girl hidden
    in the mirror. The mirror is always red.

            Red has many values. The troubadour's rose.
The whore of Babylon's red hair. The red
        you're waiting to see spill across the stage
    when I'm sawn in half.

        I like the idea of planting an idea.
    In China, red is the color for brides, & in
        the Renaissance, Mary wears red under her cloak.

        Some gods are painted red. Visible
    in the blue sky above the cannons, but not
        on the battlefield.

THE WOMAN WHO IS SAWN IN HALF THINKS ABOUT ELEPHANTS: MARIANNE MOORE FEEDING THEM BREAD AT THE CIRCUS & HOUDINI WHO MADE ONE DISAPPEAR (& WAS NOT "UNCOMFORTABLY POPULAR" WITH THEM AS WAS MISS MOORE)

All I can say about elephants, really, is that they're big.
Big & lonely.
I like them because they have big feet—big lonely
feet—& great big trunks: forty-to-a-hundred-
thousand trunk muscles.
(O, haul me, huge heart.)
My neighbor who's an eco-tourism expert tells me it takes
some time to train an elephant to carry a stranger.
My friend who reads past lives says I've always
lived in the desert.
Remember when everything had future tense?
Tromp. Tromp. Psychopomp.
Poetess with heft.
A lonely trudge, one supposes, to the perfect world.

BOX SET

—for my great-aunt Antoinette (Nettie) Bope, 1880-1902

1

Nettie in a pine box. The family Bible says *died young.* Erased.
Then written in again. *A scandal,* my mother says. Botched.
Back alley. *In all the papers.* My mother's name is Moo. *He took
advantage. Got her drunk.* My great-grandma, Nettie's mother
Susan—I'm named for her—saw a bell of fire in Nettie's shoes left
out on the landing. *Why don't you go back to teaching?* Names.
Begottens. A line of heroes, toting muskets, bugles—our ticket
to the DAR. Proper. Nettie's name erased. Who wrote it back?
Moo says *Our people didn't slight.* Men's names, doing muskety
things. No family tree for Antoinette. Antoinette (Nettie)
Bope. Frenchified Ohio. My mother's name is Moo. She told
me *everything she knows.* My name is Sudie. *Sudie, don't brood.
No one likes a gloomy puss.* Nettie has a lovely tombstone
down in Thurston.

2

Lovely tombstone down in Thurston. After the doctors and their *implements: spoons bent in different directions to suit the operation.* After weeks *convalescing* at Mrs. Beatty's, *not a place the average reputable physician would think of sending a patient.* After Nettie's father was finally notified. Called in Dr. Klous, who moved Nettie to Grant Hospital, *as I considered that a more respectable place to die.* Who did last-ditch surgery—pointless, but he *saw something.* Next day, Nettie in her coffin, at the Columbus train station—next train, Thurston. But Klous rushing to the station. Hauling her back to the hospital. Hell-bent on doing an autopsy. Why? *Daily Press*, front page, June 1, 1902: *Mysterious Circumstances Surround Girl's Death.* Klous and his autopsy. Opened her up—opened Pandora's box. Is it true Nettie wasn't pregnant?

3

Is it true Nettie wasn't pregnant? But she *thought* she was—did she try one of those mail-order concoctions? The parsley seed cure? Did it screw up her hormones? *Everybody* took them. Ads in church bulletins: *for blocked menses.* But she was seen by doctors. Hoskinson and Cookes. Did they even know how to do a pelvic exam? They *inserted implements.* Bent spoons. Penholders, *wire attached.*

                    but   *can't—*

          repeat?   1968. Baltimore. X waiting in a bar. While I go to the doctor's. To get a "rabbit test." To get a phone number so somebody could drive me someplace in Pennsylvania. Blindfolded. X had had a few beers by the time I got back to the bar. The doctor's waiting room was standing-room-only. Thick with smoke.

4

Standing-room-only. Thick. I was twenty-four. Nettie was almost twenty-two. I found her. Loved her. Made her into myself. For years, I had only one newspaper clipping: *It is said the girl was taken to the place of a Mrs. Beatty on South Pearl alley some time ago, and it was claimed she was in a delicate condition at the time.* Beatty, no first name. *Licensed midwife*, whatever that meant in 1902. But in 1902, university-trained doctors (*regular* doctors) were on a crusade to license themselves. To squeeze out the competition—the *irregulars*, like Mrs. Beatty. Who *diluted the profession*. Like me in 1976, apprentice-trained at a women's health center. For years, I had only one clipping and thought Mrs. Beatty was the abortionist. Nothing in the paper about doctors. *You don't do abortions, do you, Sue*, Moo asked me once.

5

No one should do abortions, said the regular doctors. Except themselves. Hospital boards. *Yes. No.* Checks, boxes. *Regulars* will *regulate.* Begottens. Though *concerns re preserving the stock.* Who is this Antoinette Bope? Frenchified. Farmer's daughter. Grocery clerk. *Convalescing* for weeks. Who is *the author of her ruin*? Cy Stewart? Regular docs? *Sudie, don't brood.* A student at Ohio State, Cy Stewart *claimed to know a great deal which he could tell about the girl if the press would promise not to use his name, but as he intimated it was reflections on the girl's character rather than facts in connection with the case at hand, he was informed his story was not wanted.* My white dress Emily Dickinson Nettie. Who was *hard working and held in high esteem.* Doctors and their boxes. They should've let the midwives keep the work.

6

Cookes told Dr. Klous he needed the work. Had four children. *Cried like a child. Said he took the case because he needed money to buy food. Touching appeal, but I could not promise. Monday he again asked me to protect him. At that time, however, he thought he could not be prosecuted, for the reason the girl was not gravid.* Dr. Charles F. Cookes. His colleague, Dr. Asa E. Hoskinson. Sterling Coll. grads. First names, middle initials. Regular doctors needing work. Could they tell the difference between a sixteen-week and a non-pregnant uterus? *The instrument introduced to procure the abortion had perforated the intestines and in all probability had pierced the liver.* At Mrs. Beatty's they *treated the inflamed parts with water.* No woundwort. No Keats. *It's not safe,* Moo says. *Those kooks picketing your place.*

7

Those kooks picketing. J. Kopp, from Swanton, one of our
regulars, later went down to Buffalo and shot Dr. Barnett
Slepian. Hoskinson and Cookes are going to trial. Attempted
abortion. Is the woman seeking an abortion the victim of
a crime or an accomplice? *The Daily Press* calls Nettie *the
victim of an attempt at abortion...an unfortunate young
woman...fear-stricken and misguided.* The *principals* in the
crime are the abortionist and the sexual partner. *Antoinette
Bope is dead, and somebody is responsible. Who that is must
be determined by the authorities...*

         *Dr. Hoskinson says the girl may have
caused her own death.* Nettie, on her deathbed, identified
Cookes, Hoskinson, *her seducer* Cy Stewart, and Mrs. Beatty.
But it was Nettie's brother Ed who'd hired the doctors.

8

Day after the autopsy, brother Ed *fell back into a faint* when Dr. Klous told him Nettie hadn't been pregnant. And that Ed was cleared. Ed was twenty-six. What gave Klous the authority to clear him? Did Klous want to protect him? Was Klous protecting himself? Called in by the family, guilty by association? The September 1902 *Journal of the AMA* advised physicians: *Refuse all responsibility for the patient unless a confession exonerating you from any connection to the crime is given*. What if Nettie *had* been pregnant? What if Klous said she *wasn't* pregnant to clear himself?   I didn't take the blindfolded drive in 1968—I managed to get a committee-approved abortion at Johns Hopkins Hospital. I was a Hopkins grad. One of those Hopkins perks? Hoskinson said at the trial *he assured the girl she was entertaining fears and advised her to go home.*

9

Not to worry and go home. Klous and his Pandora's box. Klous who *wanted the whole truth*. Darling of the press. Truth to what end? *Septic condition so pronounced it was of no avail*. My mother has two stories: Nettie and my grandmother, sisters a year apart. Nettie, their father's favorite. Nettie with a new red dress. Nanny a new blue dress. This is what Nanny told my mother. Why this, why *this* passed down? Nettie does something bad, their father makes them trade dresses. Second story: Nettie's been bad, and they have to trade dolls. First Hoskinson and Cookes *positively deny all knowledge of the girl or her ailment*. Then they admit to *inserting instruments*. Then beg for protection. Then, lo, story changes, Nettie's *not gravid*: they *told her to go home*. Hope for Hoskinson and Cookes. Nettie alone in her room in a white dress.

10

Nettie. All alone in a room. *Convalescing* at Mrs. Beatty's. Why wasn't malpractice on trial, not abortion? Even the Ohio State Board of Medical Registration revoked the licenses of Hoskinson and Cookes. October 9, 1902: *That the operation amounted to butchery*
septic   *so pronounced*
The doctor who taught me to do abortions at the women's health center said the big New York hospital where she'd trained had a 25-bed ward for patients with infections from illegal abortions—by 1971 when New York legalized abortion, it was empty.   After the surgery *of no avail* at Grant hospital, right before she died, Nettie told Klous *December 19 was the only time in her life*. Cy Stewart skipped town before the trial. Nettie died not knowing she wasn't pregnant.

11

Nettie died not knowing. Tell me it was a blessing. *Sudie. Sudie.* How old was Mrs. Beatty? Was she motherly? Early on, she'd said, *I try to do all the good and as little harm as I can, but I always get the worst.* Nettie's own mother put a tiny pillbox on her head, shut herself up in the parlor. Her father said, *No more girls will leave the farm.* Now my mother at 83—thirty years older than Nettie's *aged father* when he was summoned to Columbus—standing in the graveyard down at Thurston, her hair so white, wearing the white wool coat she'd bought for my wedding years ago, her black patent leather pocketbook, enormous, slung over one arm. *You don't have to lug around that purse,* I call to her. *It'll be perfectly safe in the car.* She shakes her head and takes hold of the clasp with both hands. *The Bopes are right here,* she says.

12

Right here, Moo says again, clasping the Bope family headstone, frowning slightly. Her other grandparents were her favorites. *The Bopes were a nervous bunch*, she says, *and the sisters fought like barn cats, but they were loyal to each other.* Nettie's tombstone, a few feet downslope from her parents' graves, faces away from the churchyard, in the direction of the old farm. A polished granite square wreathed with scraggly brown grass: Antoinette, Dau. of W. W. and S. L. Bope. July 7, 1880. May 30, 1902. *It's a beautiful marker*, Moo says. *Now do you feel better?* Back in the car, she looks tired, small. It's starting to drizzle. As we turn north from the cemetery out onto the main road, she looks over her shoulder and sighs. She fumbles in her purse for her compact. *Didn't you ever want children?*

13

Didn't you want children? Nettie in a white dress. Not a wedding dress. No cradle.

Nettie's mother Susan had twelve children. My grandmother was *mama* to the younger girls, killed and dressed a chicken when she was

gave up her blue   And her

No more girls will leave the farm.

Nettie *downslope.*

Klous *wanted the whole truth.* Sudie wanted the truth, too.

Missed, I almost missed it after months poring over front-page headlines. The trial. Fast forward. Rewind. Buried on page 7, *Columbus Daily Press.* Just the facts, ma'am. March 14, 1903: *Dr. Hoskinson Not Guilty. Criminal Jury Rendered Verdict—Indictment Against Dr. Cookes Nollied.*

14

Verdict: not guilty. Indictment nollied. They dug the grave. Amen. They sang—or did not sing—the Christian hymns. *Who will Carry Me over the River?* Amen. They did not preach justice. They did not preach truth. They shoveled red dirt into the hole.

Cy Stewart, the *author of Nettie's ruin*

back to town?   Ohio State?

Nettie's brother
What good to publish the facts? Facts weren't going to bring his sister back. But what were they thinking in the jury box? Nettie in a pine box. *Died young.*

15

Erased.

Nettie

died not

guilty   They dug the grave.

IV

TODAY I MUST WRITE MY OBITUARY

How do I word it, old body,
old mind? *She was born in Ohio.*

Should I say, *Nearly drowned
in Ohio.* Should I add the word *once*?

Should I say, *She matriculated, often,
she studied Dickinson in the original,
she loved her naps.*

Her life's work—teacher, abortionist:
When does human life begin? end?
She read up on ensoulment.

Should I say, *She traveled many places,
once in search of a cake no longer
made by nuns in Palermo.*

Is it obvious, *Overly
eager*?

She was married more than once,
but should I say *once*?

Should I say, *She died in her sleep.
She died open-eyed.*

She died, and someone was with her.
The soul with its elephant face.

The elephant god, red Ganesh—
friend for the journey, who clears the path:

who carries an axe to fell desires,
but holds out a sweet.

Round, with round eyes,
O, like a human face.

WHY I'M NOT COMING TO MY FUNERAL

You don't want me there.

You set out photos of another woman.

No raisins in the cake.

The night too dark, the day too hot.

The daisies in disarray.

You stood on my porch,
looking in, but didn't knock.

I opened the storm, *Do I know you?*
You said, *No.*

I said, *I have to go in now.*
You said, *Yes.*

THE WOMAN WHO IS TO BE SAWN IN HALF

Only half of the house / was haunted.
— Jon Woodward

though the issue is of
course not where the soul
is housed but where not
today like a phantom limb
& why or not tomorrow

& since when did the
snip stop paying rent O
so well done better half
keep on your red wool
thinking cap is what she

THE WOMAN WHO WAS SAWN IN HALF SENDS A MISSIVE
TO THE ONUS-SPHERE

love, you unsphered me

swerved me

unsaturned, unringed me

played Zeus and split me in two

rended me

pined me

(they say grief is a stage. death is.
your exit, stage left. your absence my
burden, my box, house in my head.
remember? remember?? we taunted
the gods: *can't keep us apart.* full
of ourselves, all sonnety, all
billet-doux coo.) then you

ALL IN ALL, ANOTHER PRODUCTIVE DAY IN THE THICKET OF DISAPPOINTMENT

My brain in a bramble, heart in a porcupine vest. & at the end of the box, a pair of Red Fox racers—hyper-extended toes, dangling chokecherries. Birds & bitter berries up there in the brain as well. Of course, the heart is a "little brain." Oxytocin & social cues. Not just a simple pump. So, for instance, if the heart races, you will feel anxious, & if you feel anxious, the heart will race. Antidotally, tickle the heart three times a week. Tickle *me*. What a lovely old-fashioned word. In my field, we say *the show must go on*—i.e., art has a mission. Well, then a broken heart is a problem.

THE WOMAN WHO IS SAWN IN HALF IS IN LOVE
WITH OLIVER SACKS

I would go up to Oliver Sacks at a party & he wouldn't
sidle away when he asked what do you do & I told him.

Oliver Sacks at 80. Mercury on the periodic table.

Now, I'm in love with Adrienne Rich. Or at least
in love with the poem that says

I touch you knowing we weren't born tomorrow—

Is it better for me to love the Adrienne Rich who built
the poem or the Adrienne Rich inside the poem?

Oliver Sacks doesn't remember faces, but he would
recognize me in a poem.

Oliver Sacks is happy to be Mercury,
solid when it's cold. He can turn on the heat

whenever he wants.

When I am 80, I will still love my box.

My box is a tooth, & I am the root.
My box edged with gold.

MY NARRATIVE BENT IS BENT ON TELLING A STORY

Chapter two. Rain. Thunder. Sleet, hail, sleazy streets.
Moon gone to the dogs. Her dress darker than the bridge
on her Blue Willow saucer. Tiny suppositions
dangling. But he finds a chip on the rim. Not as good
as it seemed. Dress the color of ice. Shade of a wrong turn.
Better add *in bed* to your fortune, cookie. He's a good
cause. She's lit up like a relationship. Silky,
slits up the side. Plot hopelessly predictable: air
all goldy, then The End & the black plastic bag
of effects. But whose effect? Shouldn't ask.
Better add *in bed* to counteract momentum. *De-lish* here
in the bakery of the mind. The pendulum theory applies
vaguely, if at all. But look: he's back, gap-toothed
& grinning. Gold carp under the ice, biting the hook.

SHOULD I TAKE IT AS A SIGN

that the *Don't Bore God* note taped
to my desk just fell to the floor,
that I dreamt you gave me
a sandwich wrapped in a glove
& I ate the glove,
that I was mortified even
in my dream?
That the pony I always wanted
I never got. Piebald.
I would've called her Cowboy.
Was that the problem?
That I feel you sweating in the night
& I'm afraid.
That I'm afraid to tell you
in the morning.
That my friend Lewis says
my name in Mandarin
is shuōbùtōng, which
means *talk no communicate.*
That Samuel Beckett
& I have the same initials.
(*Let's go. We can't. Why not?*)
Both born April 13.
That my fortune cookie says, *Bite me.*
That I hear you crying in the night.
That a shaman in the Colombian rain forest
told my friend Megan,
I've been waiting for you.
That once a psychic told me
she saw piles of paper under my desk.
That once a guy at a bar said,
Don't I know you from someplace?
That years after the funeral
my father says he misses me,
that I still see him
walking down the street.

His back always to me.
That the famous Lama said to Lar,
What took you so long?
God, I don't want to bore.
Just give me some kind of sign.

LET US CONSIDER JULIA

Let us consider Julia, who is like the U.S.,
brash, on-the-run, a mutt—Lutheran, Sufi, Jew,
though not a Methodist that doth not dance,
and not a Buddhist either, for Julia will not SIT.
Nor will Julia take vows, who worships daily in her way
the Gods of vowels and the G-ds of no vowels.
Who sheds on the lap of the Goddess.
Who daily anoints the dogwood.
Who begs at the Masters' table and feels no shame.
Who pounces on her rawhide demon.
Who trembles beneath the bed when Thunder Woman grumbles.
Who guards the door like Cerberus.
Who preaches to the birds.
Who naps.
Who puts on the dog.
Who is an instrument for cats to learn manners upon.
Who has God's good hairy nose.
Who blesses this day, February 9, for St. Tooth.
Whose tail is bent like W and therefore she is God.
Who is waggish and wiry and therefore she is God.
Who is P that introduces Pleasure and therefore she is God.
Who loves Massillon, Ohio, as St. Francis loved Assisi.
Who loves the hometown tribe the Tigers.
Who calls herself *Tyger! Tyger!*
Who sits fearsomely in the bleachers on a bright orange cushion.
Who snarls at the Canton Bulldogs and gladly would nip.
Who loves the bulldog as her kin.
Who whinnies to the Lord who scratches her ears.
Who whimpers at the sight of the forsaken mills in Massillon.
Who loves her dog's life.
Whose third cousin dated the dog in the moon.
Who vowelouls and no-vowelouls late this February night.
The Lord is great and glad.
Who swims daily in the rezy, as cleanliness is next to godliness.

Who shakes water on us all, to share her blessings.
Who chases rats in the deserted Republic Steel.
Who fears the red wolf and the red wolf's hunger.
Who would chase the rich men who deserted Republic Steel.

RUBY

They were red, with silver heels, and she took them off before she drowned so she could wear them to the wake. Her name was Ruby. Baudelaire said color thinks by itself. Ruby said red ignites the spine. Her skirt was heavy. The night was warm, almost cloudless, the kind of night where you turn down a side street and suddenly the sky is red, streaked with red, and you're not sure what time it is, if it's night or day— somebody's singing *I will always love you* and you know this time it's true.

THE TRIUMPH OF GREED

cassata comes from the Arabic *q'as at*, meaning "box"

In the box this afternoon I thought about cake. An over-the-top many-layered pistachio cream and pomegranate-filled Sicilian *cassata* called *Trionfo di Gola*. (First baked by nuns in Palermo.) *Throat Triumph*. Or the *Triumph of Gluttony*. Or, my favorite, the *Triumph of Greed*. It's a *Duomo* of desire, enrobed in pale green marzipan, it's a convex Grail. It's for my mother. And for Hades, who stole more than half a year. I am twelve again, December, snowing, afternoons my mother *takes to her bed*. Afternoons merging into weeks. My father cooks the meals. I try to cheer her up by wiggling my knees. At night I practice in front of the mirror. Demeter bitter as winter. Persephone, wrenched from here to there, a child with no say, with childlike hungers. O, Demeter, the *lack* of desire— deadly. A bone in the throat. Like god. (But wasn't the gnawing deprivation of even all those anorexic saints just another form of greed?) Like Demeter's grief. The ending of a long story, and the middle of another: Demeter laughed. And then she ate.

THE BOX

> Inside the box, Beauty.
> If you open the box, Death.
> —after *Eros & Psyche*, Apuleius

When the Maestro pulls the casket apart,
you see nothing—there is *nothing*—
a *mystery*—at the center.

His task is to confuse you.

Death is a sleight of hand—
crowds at every matinee:

Beauty, the ritual
sacrifice.

I am only human
& in the House of Illusion.

ᪿ

Nothing there but death. When he pulled me
apart. Head at one end, feet at the other.

Why did I go out there with him? Waterfalls?
Green birds in the canopies? Where was my mother?

Don't believe them when they say *things happen
for a reason*.

Black wings. Inked
on his arm.

PARING KNIFE

My appetite for onions. Their give. Their tears. Long
periods of dark, the dour regiments of forks and spoons.
Then the double-zippered pouch: coins, keys, thin gold chain,
three bottles of French perfume. Waft of citrine. The old
woman is valuable. I keep the old woman safe. I hear the
daughter in the kitchen slamming cupboards. *Why is the knife
in your purse?*

I remember the turnip's resistance. Resignation of the
cucumber. Then the luster of the nightstand drawer: slips and
straps and lace and leggings, silver foil from Hershey's Kisses,
cellophane, dimes, scissors twice my size.

Rat Stash. The daughter's fussing slithers through the
nightstand drawer like rust. *Crow's nest.*

Flurry of folding. Chittering of spoons. Then the daughter
goes away, and I go back where I belong. So much to keep in
mind, putting things in place. I was big in a dream, and keen,
a beak like a buzzard's. I hacked at the daughter's door. Knee
socks and a green checked dress. She cried. I remember. I
remember how the tomato yields.

O, my friends are sheeny papers, are tweezers and white
leather gloves. We are the valuables. The soul is in the fat,
not in the bone. The visiting nurse will steal us.

BY THE RIVERS

By the rivers of Babylon we sat down and wept: when we remembered thee, O Zion. She bobs her hands two times to say Go on. She hasn't spoken for three months. *We paused before a House that seemed a Swelling of the Ground.*

Always we. *Such a pretty girl, Daddy will bring us a present. We don't like heights, we need our sleep.* Speak for yourself, I say. She glowers at the frayed blue curtain by the bed, *Does Daddy know we're here?* Daddy's in heaven and knows everything, Daddy thinks it's pretty here. Too late now to spell it out: This is it, what we can afford. Always a dream. At eighty-seven with her pencil and her stories and her elf named Perk. *Time yet. A hundred visions and revisions. Let us go then.* Pretty when she was young. When I was young.

A hundred indecisions. Drony taking of a toast and tea. Already I spend afternoons staring at the neighbor's yard. Only grackles at the feeder now, and palsied sparrows. She will live to 100, sucking me dry. I have nothing left. My friend Ruthie washed her mother's body and laid her in straw. What could even a priest say for the spirit of her life? Chitchat for the void.

O Zion.

RINGLING BROS: MOTHER & DAUGHTER, FUNERAL PROCESSION

after Elizabeth Ernst's *The Final Act*, 2007
(printed photo linen, paint)

my mother is riding me, her little Celeste, her elephant princess,
her little fat lady tattooed in black, she rides on my back,
she wears plumes & comfy red slippers, her face painted white

she kicks her heels into my hide, but my heart is a locket—

she rides on my back, the heart is a doorway, her little fat lady
tattooed in black, she flicks her whip behind my knees,
folds of sorrow behind my knees, & we circle the ring

she kicks her heels into my hide—

we circle the ring, the heart a tattoo—*Mother* & roses—
O, my first love, the heart is an arrow, loosed from a quiver,
she wears plumes & comfy red slippers, her lips painted red

my heart is a locket—

a red satin cushion, lid of white pine, she wears plumes
& my fat lady sweater, draped like a shroud,
she kicks her heels into my side, but my heart—my heart—

I won't let you go, kicking, kicking, my sorrow, my sorrow

NOTES

THE SELBIT BOX

The *blood-thirsty... hair-raising*[1] Selbit box in which a woman is sawn in half was introduced in 1921 by the magician P. T. Selbit (with the prototypical ever-smiling magician's assistant Betty Barker inside). London. The Roaring Twenties. When this sawing took place, crowds lined up for blocks; Selbit's stage hands dumped reddened water into the gutters behind Finsbury Park Empire; nurses stood in white caps by the exits, an ambulance parked out front. As a publicity stunt, P. T. Selbit offered suffragette Christabel Pankhurst £20 a week to be his *permanent sawing block*.[2] (She declined.)

[1] Review, *Daily Express*, 1921
[2] Magic Circle's official publication, 1921
Thank you to Jim Steinmeyer for his magical research. See *Hiding the Elephant*, Carroll and Graf, 2003

BULLETPROOF

Thank you to Spencer Reece for his phrase *obscure, intimate spiritual contraptions* in "Countless Cries: Father Gerard Manley Hopkins," *The American Poetry Review*, Vol. 38/No. 5.

THE WOMAN WHO IS SAWN IN HALF THINKS ABOUT ELEPHANTS: MARIANNE MOORE FEEDING THEM BREAD AT THE CIRCUS & HOUDINI WHO MADE ONE DISAPPEAR (& WAS NOT "UNCOMFORTABLY POPULAR" WITH THEM AS WAS MISS MOORE)

In a letter to Donald Stanford, Elizabeth Bishop describes an afternoon at the circus with Marianne Moore, feeding bread to the elephants—"They like it even better than peanuts, and we were uncomfortably popular with them."

Moore herself disappeared an elephant. She left "Black Earth" out of her *Collected*.

BOX SET

The Cleveland Medical Journal

Vol 1 January 1903 No 2 Following the action of the State Board of Medical Registration and Examination which revoked the right of C. F. Cookes and Asa E. Hoskinson, of Columbus, to practice medicine on account of an alleged criminal abortion, the grand jury has found true bills against both of the above-mentioned physicians and has caused their arrest. The court has placed them each under $1,000 bonds.

Columbus Medical Journal

Vol XXVI No 10, 1902 Revocation of Licensures
Vol XXVII No 1, 1903 refused to rehear applications for recertification
Vol XXVII No 3, 1903 Hoskinson acquitted in jury trial, Cookes nollied
Vol XXVII No 8, 1903 Cookes's certificate restored

The Journal of the American Medical Association

October 1902, XXXIX Ohio Board revokes Licenses – the Ohio State Board of Medical Registration and Examination revoked the licenses of Drs. A. E. Hoskinson and Charles F. Cookes, of Columbus, October 7, for alleged criminal malpractice. It is stated that the state's attorney will follow this with prosecution in the criminal courts.

1903 Vol XL Part 1 Abortionist Sentenced.—Dr. H. Negley Teeters, Steubenville, Ohio, charged with having caused the death of Miss Grace Goodwin of Empire, by a criminal operation, pleaded guilty and was sentenced on March 3 to imprisonment for four years in the penitentiary.

June 1903, XL Asa E. Hoskinson, M.D., Sterling Medical College, Columbus, Ohio, 1883, died at his home in Columbus, May 19, from pneumonia, after an illness of two weeks, aged 45.

1905, XLV Charles F. Cookes, M.D. Sterling Medical College, Columbus, Ohio. 1882, died at his home in Columbus, November 1, from nephritis, after an illness of more than a year, aged 65.

Sue D. Burton is a physician assistant specializing in women's health care. Her poetry has appeared in *Beloit Poetry Journal, Blackbird, Green Mountains Review, Mudlark, New Ohio Review, Shenandoah*, and on *Verse Daily*. She has been awarded *Fourth Genre*'s 2017 Steinberg Essay Prize, a Vermont Arts Council grant, and nominations for the Pushcart Prize and the Best of the Net. Her chapbook *Little Steel* is forthcoming (Fomite Press). She holds degrees in writing from Johns Hopkins University and the Vermont College MFA and was apprenticeship-trained as a physician assistant at the Vermont Women's Health Center.

Publications by Two Sylvias Press:

The Daily Poet: Day-By-Day Prompts For Your Writing Practice
by Kelli Russell Agodon and Martha Silano (Print and eBook)

The Daily Poet Companion Journal (Print)

Fire On Her Tongue: An Anthology of Contemporary Women's Poetry
edited by Kelli Russell Agodon and Annette Spaulding-Convy (Print and eBook)

The Poet Tarot and Guidebook: A Deck Of Creative Exploration (Print)

Box, Winner of the Two Sylvias Press 2017 Poetry Book Prize
by Sue D. Burton (Print and eBook)

Tsigan: The Gypsy Poem (2nd Edition)
by Cecilia Woloch (Print and eBook)

PR For Poets: A Guidebook To Publicity And Marketing
by Jeannine Hall Gailey (Print and eBook)

Appalachians Run Amok, Winner of the 2016 Two Sylvias Press Wilder Prize
by Adrian Blevins (Print and eBook)

Killing Marias
by Claudia Castro Luna (Print and eBook)

The Ego and the Empiricist, Finalist 2016 Two Sylvias Press Chapbook Prize
by Derek Mong (Print and eBook)

The Authenticity Experiment
by Kate Carroll de Gutes (Print and eBook)

Mytheria, Finalist 2015 Two Sylvias Press Wilder Prize
by Molly Tenenbaum (Print and eBook)

Arab in Newsland , Winner of the 2016 Two Sylvias Press Chapbook Prize
by Lena Khalaf Tuffaha (Print and eBook)

The Blue Black Wet of Wood, Winner of the 2015 Two Sylvias Press Wilder Prize
by Carmen R. Gillespie (Print and eBook)

Fire Girl: Essays on India, America, and the In-Between
by Sayantani Dasgupta (Print and eBook)

Blood Song
by Michael Schmeltzer (Print and eBook)

Naming The No-Name Woman,
Winner of the 2015 Two Sylvias Press Chapbook Prize
by Jasmine An (Print and eBook)

Community Chest
by Natalie Serber (Print)

Phantom Son: A Mother's Story of Surrender
by Sharon Estill Taylor (Print and eBook)

What The Truth Tastes Like
by Martha Silano (Print and eBook)

landscape/heartbreak
by Michelle Peñaloza (Print and eBook)

Earth, Winner of the 2014 Two Sylvias Press Chapbook Prize
by Cecilia Woloch (Print and eBook)

The Cardiologist's Daughter
by Natasha Kochicheril Moni (Print and eBook)

She Returns to the Floating World
by Jeannine Hall Gailey (Print and eBook)

Hourglass Museum
by Kelli Russell Agodon (eBook)

Cloud Pharmacy
by Susan Rich (eBook)

Dear Alzheimer's: A Caregiver's Diary & Poems
by Esther Altshul Helfgott (eBook)

Listening to Mozart: Poems of Alzheimer's
by Esther Altshul Helfgott (eBook)

*Crab Creek Review 30th Anniversary Issue featuring Northwest Poets*edited by
Kelli Russell Agodon and Annette Spaulding-Convy (eBook)

Please visit Two Sylvias Press (www.twosylviaspress.com) for information on
purchasing our print books, eBooks, writing tools, and for submission guidelines
for our annual book prizes. Two Sylvias Press also offers editing services and
manuscript consultations.

Created with the belief that great writing is good for the world.
Visit us online: www.twosylviaspress.com

CPSIA information can be obtained
at www.ICGtesting.com
Printed in the USA
FFHW02n2147250918
48571090-52474FF